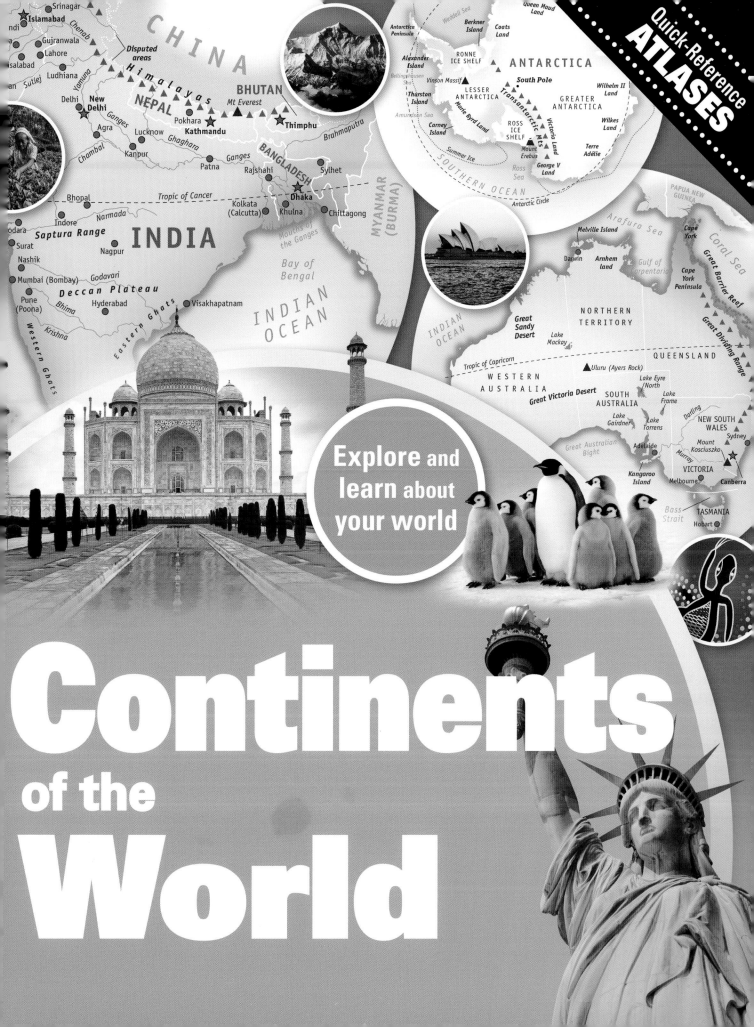

Explore and learn about your world

Continents
of the
World

Author:
Toby Reynolds

Editorial director:
Kathy Middleton

Editor:
Wendy Scavuzzo

Proofreader:
Rodelinde Albrecht

Cover and interior design:
Green Android Ltd

Print and production coordinator:
Katherine Berti

Images © shutterstock.com: aand aunes © N Mrtgh; aboriginal vase © Philippe Put; acropolis © polartern; ala-archa © gopixgo; amber © Alexander Hoffmann; angel falls © Lysithee; angkor wat © Nestor Noci; asian elephant and calf © Mogens Trolle; bab agnaou © Philip Lange; bald eagle © Paul Barnwell; bananas © Gualberto Becerra; banff national park © Douglas Wielfaert; baseball and bat © Fotoline; bayan zagH © Louise Cukrov; bengal tiger © neelsky; black-forest © a9photo; bolshoi ballet © Sergey Petrov; broken hill © Lauren Cameo; brown bear © Stayer; buckingham palace © Renata Sedmakova; budapest and the Danube © Kochneva Tetyana; bullet train © Thomas Nord; caminito street © Anibal Trejo; caribbean flamingo © Pablo H Caridad; caviar © tarasov; chichen Itza © holbox; chocolate © Ronald Sumners; christ the redeemer © Celso Pupo; cinnamon © Preto Perola; CN Tower © Elena Elisseeva; cocoa pods © Norman Chan; coconut © Maks Narodenko; coffee © Gyorgy Barna; colosseum © unknown1861; cricket © woodsy; death valley © Ihervas; diamonds © Denis Vrublevski; djavolja varos © Slobodan Djajic; dombra © Veniamin Kraskov; eiffel tower © Jose Ignacio Soto; elephant seal © elephant seal; fiji beach © fritz16; forest © Ma Spitz; galapagos tortoise © Michael Zysman; galo de barcelos © Lusoimages; ganges river © suronin; giant pandas © Cupertino; giant swallowtail butterfly © James Laurie; giant's causeway © Joe Gough; gizah pyramids © Andresr; grand canyon © Pixelite; great barrier reef © tororo reaction; great wall of china © qingqing; guiana space centre © amskad; gymnast © konstantynov; halloumi © Martin Turzak; halong bay © Le Do; hamer woman © Hector Conesa; hockey © Ryan Morgan; hong baos © WICHAN KONGCHAN; iberian lynx © Ivan Montero Martinez; igloo © Rita Januskeviciute; jazz player © Rick Lord; kaaba mecca © Sufi; kamchatka volcano © Milevshi; kangaroo © Rafael Ramirez Lee; lake baikal © Oleg Gekman; laksa © Lim Yong Hian; logs © 2009fotofriends; lotus temple © Aleksandar Todorovic; macaque © Rickshu; machu picchu © Jarno Gonzalez Zarraonandia; mamallapuram © Aleksandar Todorovic; maple leaf © Melinda Fawver; maple syrup © marilyn barbone; monastery in petra © Aleksandar Todorovic; morelia cathedral © Natursports; mount everest © Galyna Andrushko; mount fuji © Neale Cousland; mount kilimanjaro © Graeme Shannon; mountain © vichie81; Mozart statue © gary718; namsan tower © JinYoung Lee; Native American © Joseph Sohm; niagara falls © Ronald Sumners; northern lights © James Thew; nou camp stadium © Natursports; oil refinery © Marafona; orangutan © Burhan Bunardi Xie; paddy field © LIN, CHUN–TSO; pamukkale © gallimaufry; Panama Canal © Chris Jenner; pasta © ultimathule; peacock © defpicture; penguins © penguins; peter the great © Roman Gorielov; petronas twin towers © Vitaly Titov & Maria Sidelnikova; plov © Lisovskaya Natalia; polar bears © Uryadnikov Sergey; popocatepetl volcano © Marco Regalia; redwood trees © urosr; research station © Armin Rose; rio de janeiro carnival © gary yim; rugby © Jouke van Keulen; saffron © B Calkins; saguaro cactus © MBoe; sahara desert © Pichugin Dmitry; sea ice © Gentoo Multimedia Ltd; sea turtle © holbox; shark © Willyam Bradberry; sheep © Dmitry Naumov; siberian tiger© S.R. Maglione; ski jumper © Martin Lehmann; sky above sea © kanate; snow leopard © Krzysztof Wiktor; snowboarder © Dmitriy Shironosov; sognefjord © F.C.G.; songfestival © Irene Teesalu; songkran © swissmacky; springbok © Wendy Nero; st. basil's cathedral © Valery Shanin; statue of liberty © JIANHAO GUAN; steel drum musician © Lisa F. Young; sugar beet © Maksud; sultan omar ali saifuddin mosque © ppart; sunflower © Valentina_S; sydney opera house © my-summit; taj mahal © Waj; taman negara © faberfoto; the white house © James Steidl; tram © Ivo Brezina; trans-siberian railway © russal; triglav national park © Vaclav Volrab; tv © MishAl; vanilla © kschrei; vatnajokull glacier © sergioboccardo; viking ship dragon head © Alfio Ferlito; wheat © Elena Elisseeva; white wagtail © Cristian Mihai; wind turbines © TebNad; windmill © NREY; winterlude © Vlad Ghiea; woman at venice carnival © Luboslav Tiles; woman.frompapuan tribe © Byelikova Oksana; women pick tea leafs © PavelSvoboda; yugyd va national park © Fokin Oleg; yurt © Pete Niesen; zebra © ale_rizzo.

Library and Archives Canada Cataloguing in Publication

Reynolds, Toby, author
    Continents of the world / Toby Reynolds.

(Quick-reference atlases)
Includes index.
Issued in print and electronic formats.
ISBN 978-0-7787-5039-0 (hardcover).--
ISBN 978-0-7787-5049-9 (softcover).--
ISBN 978-1-4271-2148-6 (HTML)

    1. Continents--Juvenile literature. 2. Geography--Miscellanea--Juvenile literature. I. Title.

G133.R49 2018   j910.914'1   C2018-902485-2
                                   C2018-902486-0

Library of Congress Cataloging-in-Publication Data

Names: Reynolds, Toby., author
Title: Continents of the world / Toby Reynolds.
Description: New York : Crabtree Publishing Company, 2019. |
    Series: Quick-reference atlases | Includes index.
Identifiers: LCCN 2018021428 (print) | LCCN 2018029950 (ebook) |
    ISBN 9781427121486 (Electronic) |
    ISBN 9780778750390 (hardcover) |
    ISBN 9780778750499 (pbk)
Subjects: LCSH: Atlases. | LCGFT: World atlases.
Classification: LCC G1021 (ebook) | LCC G1021 .R597 2019 (print) |
    DDC 912--dc23
LC record available at https://lccn.loc.gov/2018021428

Crabtree Publishing Company

www.crabtreebooks.com   1-800-387-7650
Published in 2019 by Crabtree Publishing Company

First published in Great Britain in 2013 by Green Android Ltd
Copyright © Green Android Ltd 2013

Published in Canada
Crabtree Publishing
616 Welland Ave.
St. Catharines, Ontario
L2M 5V6

Published in the United States
Crabtree Publishing
PMB 59051
350 Fifth Avenue, 59th Floor
New York, New York 10118

Created and produced by:
Green Android Ltd
49 Beaumont Court
Upper Clapton Road
London E5 8BG
United Kingdom
www.greenandroid.co.uk

Please note that every effort has been made to check the accuracy of the information contained in this book, and to credit the copyright holders correctly. Green Android Ltd apologise for any unintentional errors or omissions, and would be happy to include revisions to content and/or acknowledgements in subsequent editions of this book.

Printed in the U.S.A./082018/CG20180601

About this atlas

This *World Atlas* has been arranged by continents. Each page is filled with maps, photographs, information, and facts. Learn about the people, places, wildlife, and famous landmarks that can be found in each of the world's regions. From the very hottest, driest desert to the cold, icy lands of the Antarctic, you will discover more about our fascinating world and its amazing features.

Key to the maps

Use the **symbols** below to identify capital cities, major towns, borders, and main geographical features.

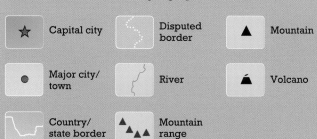

☆ Capital city

● Major city/ town

Country/ state border

Disputed border

River

Mountain range

▲ Mountain

▲ Volcano

Contents

About the world

There are seven continents and five major oceans in the world. Oceans cover 71 percent of the globe. The rest is land or ice. The Arctic and Antarctic poles receive no direct sunlight, so they are very cold. Moving south or north from each pole, temperatures increase, reaching their highest between the tropics of Cancer and Capricorn at the equator. Between each pole and its nearest tropic, the climate is subtropical or temperate.

Map of the continents

North America · Europe · Asia · Africa · South America · Australasia and Oceania · Antarctica

Environments of the world

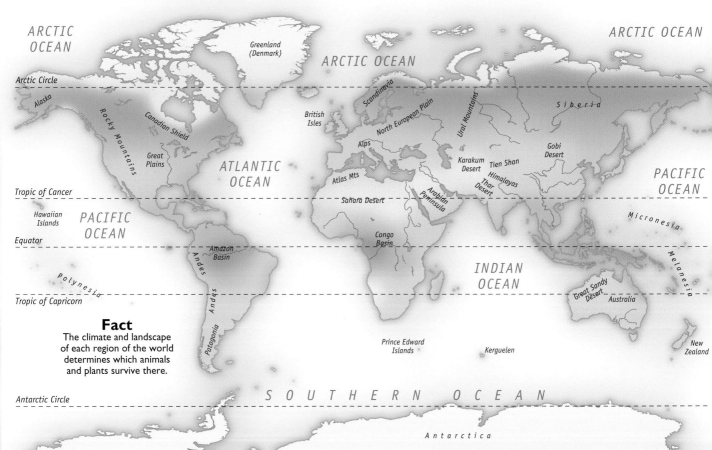

ARCTIC OCEAN
Greenland (Denmark)
ARCTIC OCEAN
ARCTIC OCEAN
Arctic Circle
Alaska
Rocky Mountains
Canadian Shield
Great Plains
British Isles
Scandinavia
North European Plain
Ural Mountains
Siberia
Alps
Atlas Mts
Karakum Desert
Tien Shan
Gobi Desert
Himalayas
Thar Desert
Arabian Peninsula
ATLANTIC OCEAN
Sahara Desert
Tropic of Cancer
Hawaiian Islands
PACIFIC OCEAN
PACIFIC OCEAN
Micronesia
Equator
Congo Basin
Amazon Basin
Andes
INDIAN OCEAN
Melanesia
Polynesia
Great Sandy Desert
Australia
Tropic of Capricorn
New Zealand
Patagonia
Prince Edward Islands
Kerguelen
Antarctic Circle
SOUTHERN OCEAN
Antarctica

Fact
The climate and landscape of each region of the world determines which animals and plants survive there.

Deserts

Deserts are bare and dry places. They can be very hot or icy cold. Some are both and vary from day to night.

Oceans

There are five major oceans of the world. Oceans cover more than two-thirds of the world's surface.

Forests

Forests are areas with a high density of trees. They can be hot and wet in the tropics, or milder elsewhere.

Snow and ice

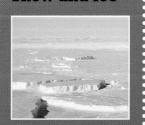

The coldest parts of the world are in the very north and south. These areas are made up of ice and snow.

Mountains

Mountain ranges get colder the higher you climb. Few animals can survive at the very top of high mountains.

Antarctica and the Arctic

The most northern part of the world is called the Arctic. Although there is little land there, a huge frozen ocean creates an icy landscape. Antarctica is the most southerly region of the world and is an enormous ice-covered continent. These icy landscapes are at opposite ends of the world. Whales and seals are some of the very few animals that can survive in the low temperatures of both the Antarctic and the Arctic.

Industry and technology

1

The only people who live in Antarctica are the scientists and staff in research stations. These stations were created to study the icy environment and **exceptional** nature of this frozen land.

Research station

Nature and wildlife

2

Emperor penguins are the biggest species of penguin. They are the only animals to spend winter on Antarctica's ice. They live on a diet of fish and shellfish, such as squid and **krill**.

Emperor penguins

Fact
The thickest ice in the world is at Wilkes Land. The ice there can be nearly 3 miles (5 km) deep.

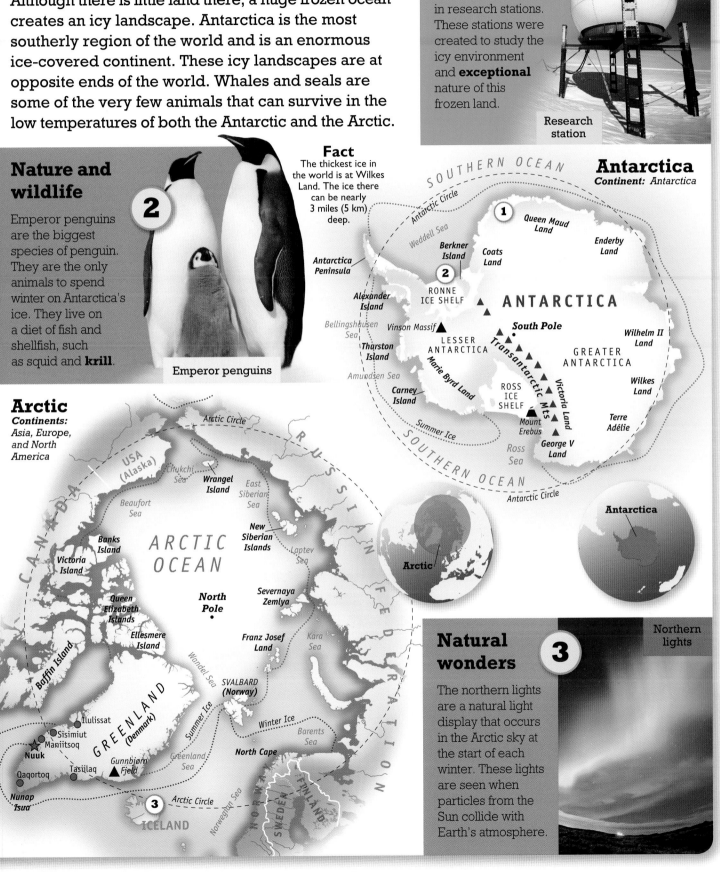

Antarctica
Continent: *Antarctica*

SOUTHERN OCEAN
Antarctic Circle
Weddell Sea
Queen Maud Land
Enderby Land
1
Berkner Island
Coats Land
Antarctica Peninsula
2
RONNE ICE SHELF
ANTARCTICA
Alexander Island
Bellingshausen Sea
Vinson Massif
LESSER ANTARCTICA
South Pole
Transantarctic Mts
GREATER ANTARCTICA
Wilhelm II Land
Thurston Island
Marie Byrd Land
Victoria Land
Wilkes Land
Amundsen Sea
Carney Island
ROSS ICE SHELF
Summer Ice
Mount Erebus
Terre Adélie
George V Land
Ross Sea
SOUTHERN OCEAN
Antarctic Circle

Arctic
Continents: *Asia, Europe, and North America*

Arctic Circle
CANADA
USA (Alaska)
Chukchi Sea
Wrangel Island
East Siberian Sea
RUSSIAN FEDERATION
Beaufort Sea
Banks Island
New Siberian Islands
Laptev Sea
Victoria Island
ARCTIC OCEAN
Queen Elizabeth Islands
North Pole
Severnaya Zemlya
Ellesmere Island
Franz Josef Land
Kara Sea
Baffin Island
Wandel Sea
SVALBARD (Norway)
Ilulissat
Sisimiut
Maniitsoq
Nuuk
GREENLAND (Denmark)
Summer Ice
Winter Ice
Barents Sea
Tasiilaq
Qaqortoq
Gunnbjørn Fjeld
Greenland Sea
North Cape
Nunap Isua
Arctic Circle
NORWAY
SWEDEN
FINLAND
Norwegian Sea
ICELAND
3

Arctic

Antarctica

Natural wonders

3

The northern lights are a natural light display that occurs in the Arctic sky at the start of each winter. These lights are seen when particles from the Sun collide with Earth's atmosphere.

Northern lights

Canada

Canada is the second-largest country in the world. It is known for the four Great Lakes on the border with the United States (another lies entirely in the USA.) Around 400 years ago, British and French settlers made Canada their home. **Descendants** of these settlers make up about half of the population. There are many different groups of **Indigenous** Canadians. These include Inuit peoples who live in the Arctic regions of Canada.

Ancient world

Inuit peoples settled in Canada's northern region in 1050 CE. To aid hunting, they built stone monuments, called **inuksuit**, as **navigation aids**. Inuksuit with a head, legs, and arms (*inunnguaq*) have a **symbolic** meaning.

Inunnguaq

Banff National Park

National parks

Banff National Park was established in 1885. It was the first National Park in Canada. The town of Banff is 4,537 feet (1,383 m) above **sea level**, which makes it the highest city in the country.

NUMBER OF PROVINCES AND TERRITORIES
13

Sports and leisure

The Montréal Canadiens are one of Canada's best-loved ice hockey teams. This fast-paced game is played by two teams of six skaters who use sticks to shoot a small rubber disk, called a puck, into the opponent's net.

Economy and environment

Forests cover about two-thirds of British Columbia, and logging is very important for Canada's **economy**. Trees are cut down and sawed into planks or milled into paper for **export** around the world.

Logging

Natural wonders

Niagara Falls is the world's second-largest waterfall. Water from the falls flows into the Niagara River, through Lake Ontario, then down the St. Lawrence River and into the Atlantic Ocean.

Montréal Canadiens

Niagara Falls

Nature and wildlife (6)

Nunavut is home to more than half the world's polar bears. They are amazing swimmers and can swim for up to 100 miles (160 km). These bears are the largest **predators** on land. They mainly feed on ringed and bearded seals.

Polar bear

Food and drink (7)

The province of Quebec produces more maple syrup than any other. This sweet syrup is made from the sap of sugar maple, red maple, or black maple trees. It is often eaten with waffles, pancakes, or porridge.

Maple syrup

Music and festivals (8)

The Winterlude festival takes place in Ottawa each year. Ice sculptures, musical concerts, and ice skating on the frozen Rideau Canal are just some of the fun activities that take place.

Winterlude

National symbols (9)

The maple leaf is the national symbol of Canada. The leaf is shown on the Canadian flag and on many national sports teams' uniforms and company logos. There are ten **native** species of maple trees in Canada.

Maple leaf

Important buildings (10)

The CN Tower in Toronto stands 1,814 feet (553 m) tall. When the tower was completed in 1976, it was the tallest freestanding structure in the world. It was built as a communications and observation tower.

CN Tower in Toronto

Ellesmere Island

G R E E N L A N D (Denmark)

Baffin Bay

lizabeth Islands

Arctic Circle

(6)

Baffin Island

Davis Strait

N U N A V U T

Iqaluit

Hudson Strait

Southampton Island

Ungava Bay

Labrador Sea

ATLANTIC OCEAN

Hudson Bay

NEWFOUNDLAND AND LABRADOR

A

A

QUEBEC

Smallwood Reservoir

Newfoundland

Canadian Shield

MANITOBA

St. John's

Anticosti Island

ST. PIERRE & MIQUELON

Churchill

Nelson

James Bay

(9)

PRINCE EDWARD ISLAND

Gulf of St. Lawrence

Lake Winnipeg

Charlottetown

ONTARIO

NEW BRUNSWICK

(7)

Lake of the Woods

Lake Nipigon

Québec

NOVA SCOTIA

Winnipeg

Montreal

Fredericton

Halifax

Lake Huron

St. Lawrence

Lake Superior

(8) ★ Ottawa

(10) Toronto

ATLANTIC OCEAN

UNITED STATES OF AMERICA

(5)

Lake Ontario

Niagara Falls

Lake Erie

Lake Michigan

Fact
Lake Superior is the world's largest freshwater lake. It is 348 miles (560 km) from west to east and 162 miles (260 km) from north to south.

United States of America

The United States of America (USA) is one of the richest and most powerful countries in the world. The American flag has 50 stars (one for each of the states) and 13 stripes (representing each of the original colonies). The landscape changes across this huge country, from tropical beaches in Florida to high peaks in the Rocky Mountains. In the west are prairie lands and deserts, while the north has dense wilderness areas.

5 National parks

The northern coast of California has beautiful redwood forests. These trees are among the tallest and largest on Earth. They can grow to 379 feet (116 m) tall. Some of these huge trees are said to be more than 2,000 years old.

Redwood trees

1 National symbols

The bald eagle was named as the symbol of the USA in 1782. It was chosen because of the bird's long life, great strength, and majestic looks. The largest population of bald eagles is found in Alaska.

American bald eagle

People and culture

Indigenous peoples lived in North America long before European settlers arrived. Today, many Indigenous peoples live in the Navajo Nation, a territory covering parts of Arizona, Utah, and New Mexico.

2 Nature and wildlife

Huge saguaro cacti grow in the Sonoran Desert. They can reach a height of more than 42 feet (13 m) and some are more than 150 years old! The prickly saguaro is North America's largest cactus.

Saguaro cactus

4

Indigenous person

3 Natural wonders

The Grand Canyon is a vast canyon that was created over millions of years of **geological activity** and **erosion** by the Colorado River. The canyon is 277 miles (446 km) long and 18 miles (29 km) wide.

Grand Canyon

6. Farming and agriculture

Farms in the Great Plains grow more wheat than anywhere else in the world. The wheat is stored in huge grain elevators, nicknamed "prairie skyscrapers," before being shipped out by railroad or truck.

Wheat field

7. Music and festivals

Traditional jazz music or "Dixieland" is a style of jazz that was created in the city of New Orleans around 100 years ago. Each year, the city celebrates its musical history with a huge jazz festival.

Jazz in New Orleans

Famous landmarks

The Statue of Liberty represents Libertas, the Roman goddess of freedom. It was a gift to the USA from the people of France. This huge statue is located in New York Harbor on Liberty Island.

Fact

Washington, D.C., is the capital of the USA. It is named after the first president of the United States, George Washington.

The Statue of Liberty

9. Sport and leisure

Baseball is one of the most popular sports in the USA. It is played with a leather ball and wooden bat. The home of one famous team, the Red Sox, is Fenway Park in Boston, the capital of Massachusetts.

Fenway Park

Important buildings

The White House in Washington, D.C., is the official workplace and home of the president of the USA. The house took eight years to build and was finally finished in 1800. It has six floors, 132 rooms, and 35 restrooms!

Map labels

Lake of the Woods
Lake Superior
Lake Michigan
Lake Huron
Lake Ontario
Lake Erie
VERMONT
NORTH DAKOTA
Bismarck
MINNESOTA
Mississippi
WISCONSIN
MICHIGAN
NEW YORK
MAINE
Augusta
Montpelier
NEW HAMPSHIRE
Boston
MASSACHUSETTS
RHODE ISLAND
CONNECTICUT
NEW JERSEY
DELAWARE
MARYLAND
Washington D.C.
UTH DAKOTA
Pierre
St Paul
IOWA
Des Moines
Madison
Lansing
Chicago
ILLINOIS
INDIANA
OHIO
Columbus
PENNSYLVANIA
New York City
TATES
NEBRASKA
Lincoln
Springfield
Indianapolis
WEST VIRGINIA
Frankfort
VIRGINIA
KANSAS
Topeka
MISSOURI
Jefferson City
Ohio
KENTUCKY
Appalachian Mts
NORTH CAROLINA
RICA
OKLAHOMA
ARKANSAS
Nashville
TENNESSEE
SOUTH CAROLINA
Oklahoma City
Arkansas
Little Rock
MISSISSIPPI
ALABAMA
Atlanta
GEORGIA
Dallas
TEXAS
LOUISANA
Montgomery
ATLANTIC OCEAN
Austin
Houston
Jackson
Tallahassee
FLORIDA
Baton Rouge
New Orleans
Rio Grande
Gulf of Mexico
Lake Okeechobee
Miami

NUMBER OF STATES 50

North portico of the White House

Mexico and Central America

Mexico is the most southern country in North America and is famous for tropical forests, deserts, and active volcanoes. South of Mexico are the countries of Central America. This region has ideal conditions for farming bananas, sugarcane, and cotton. Farther east are the islands of the Caribbean. The clear blue waters and white sandy beaches make these islands very popular with tourists from all over the world.

Natural wonders **5**

Popocatépetl is an active volcano and the second-highest peak in Mexico. It is 17,802 feet (5,426 m) tall. In 2017, "Poco" erupted three times in two hours, throwing debris up to 0.6 miles (1 km) away.

Popocatépetl volcano

Morelia Cathedral

1 Famous landmarks

Every Saturday night, a fireworks and musical spectacle takes place outside the cathedral that dates to 1660, in the city of Morelia in Mexico. The huge towers of the Morelia Cathedral can be seen throughout the city.

N

NUMBER OF COUNTRIES
21

UNITED STATES OF AMERICA

Mexicali **3**

Ciudad Juarez

2

Chihuahua

Yaqui

Chihuahuan Desert

Río Grande

Conchos

Monterrey

Sierra Madre Occidental

Baja California

Gulf of California

Culiacán

MEXICO

Laguna Madre

San Luis Potosi

Guadalajara

Mexico City **1**

Bay of Campeche

Veracruz

Popocatépetl
Balsas
Citlaltépetl

5

Isthmus of Tehuantepec

Acapulco

Gulf of Tehuantepec

PACIFIC OCEAN

Nature and wildlife

The Gulf of California has been described as the world's aquarium because of its amazing marine life. The protected green turtles found in Gulf water grow to 3 feet (1 m) long and can live to 80 years old.

Industry and technology **3**

Mexico manufactures more LCD, LED, and flat-screen plasma televisions than any other country. Many of the electronics factories are based around Tijuana, which is close to the border of California in the USA.

Plasma television

Green turtle

2

Ancient world **4**

Chichen Itza is an archaeological site in Mexico. The Temple of Kukulkan is the largest and most important at the site. This pyramid was built on top of a previous temple between 700 and 900 years ago.

Temple of Kukulkan

National symbols

6

The national bird of the Bahamas is the flamingo. These beautiful birds are found throughout the islands. They are shy animals that like to live in remote, quiet places such as deserted islands and shorelines.

Caribbean flamingo

Economy and environment

7

The 50-mile (80-km) Panama Canal was built to make it safer and easier for ships to sail between the Pacific and Atlantic Oceans, so they no longer had to sail all the way around South America.

The Panama Canal

People and culture

Steelpans are drums made from 55-gallon (208-liter) containers that once stored oil. These instruments were first made on the islands of Trinidad and Tobago. Music that is played on them is called calypso.

8

Steelpan drummer

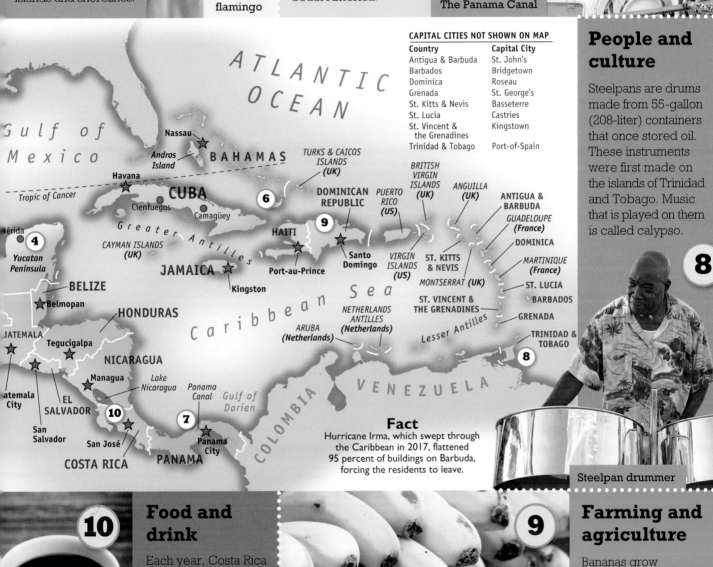

CAPITAL CITIES NOT SHOWN ON MAP

Country	Capital City
Antigua & Barbuda	St. John's
Barbados	Bridgetown
Dominica	Roseau
Grenada	St. George's
St. Kitts & Nevis	Basseterre
St. Lucia	Castries
St. Vincent & the Grenadines	Kingstown
Trinidad & Tobago	Port-of-Spain

ATLANTIC OCEAN

Gulf of Mexico

Nassau

Andros Island

BAHAMAS

Havana

Tropic of Cancer

CUBA

6

Cienfuegos

Camagüey

TURKS & CAICOS ISLANDS (UK)

DOMINICAN REPUBLIC

PUERTO RICO (US)

BRITISH VIRGIN ISLANDS (UK)

ANGUILLA (UK)

9

Greater Antilles

CAYMAN ISLANDS (UK)

HAITI

Mérida

4

Yucatan Peninsula

JAMAICA

Port-au-Prince

Santo Domingo

VIRGIN ISLANDS (US)

ST. KITTS & NEVIS

ANTIGUA & BARBUDA

GUADELOUPE (France)

DOMINICA

MARTINIQUE (France)

ST. LUCIA

BARBADOS

GRENADA

TRINIDAD & TOBAGO

8

Kingston

BELIZE

Belmopan

HONDURAS

Caribbean Sea

MONTSERRAT (UK)

ST. VINCENT & THE GRENADINES

Lesser Antilles

GUATEMALA

Tegucigalpa

NETHERLANDS ANTILLES (Netherlands)

ARUBA (Netherlands)

Guatemala City

NICARAGUA

Managua

Lake Nicaragua

EL SALVADOR

10

San Salvador

San José

COSTA RICA

Panama Canal

Gulf of Darien

7

Panama City

PANAMA

COLOMBIA

VENEZUELA

Fact
Hurricane Irma, which swept through the Caribbean in 2017, flattened 95 percent of buildings on Barbuda, forcing the residents to leave.

Food and drink

10

Each year, Costa Rica has National Coffee Day. This celebrates the great-tasting coffee that the country produces and exports around the world. This export is important to Costa Rica's economy.

Coffee

9

Bananas

Farming and agriculture

Bananas grow throughout the Caribbean region. They are harvested and exported when still green. The bananas are then ripened in rooms under special conditions until the skin turns yellow.

South America

South America is dominated by the Andes and the Amazon rain forest. The Andes form the world's longest mountain range. They are 4,350 miles (7,000 km) long and pass through seven countries. The Amazon rain forest is the world's largest rain forest and covers most of central South America. Most of the rain forest is in Brazil, but it also reaches into parts of Bolivia, Colombia, Ecuador, Guyana, Peru, Suriname, and Venezuela.

Natural wonders

1

Angel Falls, the world's highest uninterrupted waterfall, is in the Guiana Highlands, Venezuela. The 3,212-foot (989-m) falls are surrounded by cliffs and thick jungle and can only be reached by boat or plane.

Angel Falls

Ancient world

2

The city of Machu Picchu was built by the Inca people. It was abandoned in 1572 and not discovered again until 1911. The ruins of this large city are now Peru's top tourist attraction.

City of Machu Picchu

Caribbean Sea

Maracaibo • Caracas ★

VENEZUELA

Medellín • Cúcuta ▲

Orinoco

★ Bogotá

Angel Falls

COLOMBIA

N

ECUADOR

3

Equator

4 ★ Quito

Amazo

Basi

Iquitos •

GALÁPAGOS ISLANDS (Ecuador)

Piura •

PERU

Purus

Trujillo •

Ucayali

★ Lima

2 *Lake Titicaca*

BOLIV

El Misti ▲ ★ La Paz

6 Andes ★ Suc

Antofagasta •

Salt

▲ *Nevado Ojos del Salado*

Cerro Aconcagua ▲

CHILE

Santiago ★

A R G E N T I N

Concepción •

Colora

Temuco •

Chiloé Island

PACIFIC OCEAN

Andes

Patagonia

Tie de Fue

5

Straight of Magellan

Cape Ho

National parks

3

The 20 islands of Ecuador's Galápagos Islands contain unique wildlife. This Pacific Ocean **archipelago** national park is home to the world's largest tortoise and longest-lived vertebrate. An average lifespan is 100 years!

Galápagos tortoise

Farming and agriculture

4

Ecuador is known for the cocoa trees that thrive in its humid climate. The pods from the trees are roasted, then ground. When this paste is mixed with cocoa butter and sugar, chocolate is made!

Cocoa pods

Nature and wildlife

Southern elephant seals can be found on the coastline of Argentina. They are the largest of all seals. They can hold their breath for up to two hours to catch their favorite food of squid and fish.

Southern elephant seal

5

6

Deserts of the world

The Atacama Desert, which runs from Peru's southern border into northern Chile, is the driest place on Earth. Some areas never receive rain; others get up to 0.12 inches (3 mm) a year.

Atacama Desert

ATLANTIC OCEAN

Georgetown
Paramaribo
Cayenne
GUYANA
SURINAME
8
FRENCH GUIANA (France)
Marajó Island

Amazon
Belém
Manaus
Madeira
Tapajós
Fortaleza

BRAZIL

Xingu
Araguaia
Tocantins
São Francisco
Recife

Paraná
Brasília
Brazilian Highlands
Salvador

Belo Horizonte
São Paulo
9
Rio de Janeiro
10

PARAGUAY
Iguazá Falls
Asunción
Uruguay
Curitiba
Tropic of Capricorn

URUGUAY
Rosario
Lagoa dos patos
Montevideo
7
Buenos Aires
Mar del Plata

ATLANTIC OCEAN

NUMBER OF COUNTRIES 12

Fact
The Amazon River contains more water than any other river in the world. It accounts for one-fifth of the world's fresh water.

FALKLAND ISLANDS (UK)

SOUTH GEORGIA (UK)

People and culture

In Buenos Aires, a street museum called *Caminito* shows Argentina's history. Caminito means "little path" in Spanish. In the 1880s, the Italian immigrants there built and painted their houses using any materials discarded by the nearby shipyards where they worked.

7

A Caminito street

Industry and technology

The Guiana Space Centre is located at Kourou in French Guiana. The space center launches spacecraft and satellites for many countries, including the USA, Japan, Canada, India, and Brazil.

8

Guiana Space Centre

Christ the Redeemer

Famous landmarks

9

Overlooking the city of Rio de Janeiro in Brazil is a huge statue of Jesus Christ. Named *Christ the Redeemer*, it has become a very famous symbol of the city and for the whole of Brazil.

Music and festivals

10

Each year, a giant carnival takes place in Rio de Janeiro, Brazil. More than one million tourists join the city's residents for the most fantastic party that lasts for several days and several nights.

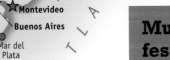

Rio Carnival

Africa

Africa lies across the equator, making it one of the hottest places on Earth. The enormous Sahara Desert separates North Africa from the rest of the continent. Rainfall is higher to the south of the Sahara, which creates vast rain forests and grasslands where wild animals such as chimpanzees, lions, and zebras are found. South Africa is popular with tourists for its beautiful mountains, lakes, and sandy beaches.

Famous landmarks

1

Bab Agnaou is one of the 19 gates that surround the ancient Moroccan city of Marrakech. The gates were built more than 800 years ago and feature **ornate** shell and floral patterns and religious **inscriptions**.

Bab Agnaou gate

2 Nature and wildlife

To protect Ghana's wildlife, the country has set aside 21 areas as national parks and reserves. In Kakum National Park, there are about 650 species of butterflies, including the giant swallowtail.

Giant swallowtail butterfly

Deserts of the world

The Sahara is the largest desert in Africa. In summer, temperatures can reach 117 °F (47 °C), but a winter's night can be below 32 °F (0 °C). Plants and animals have to be highly adapted to survive in this habitat.

3

Sahara Desert

Industry and technology

In 1967, a huge amount of diamonds was discovered at the edge of the Kalahari Desert in Botswana. Diamond mines were developed and Botswana became a top producer of fine diamonds.

Diamonds

4

National symbols

The national animal of South Africa is the springbok. It is known for its habit of leaping (correctly called pronking). With back arched and legs stiff, it can pronk 6.6 feet (2 m) above the ground.

5

Springbok

NUMBER OF COUNTRIES
54

Fact
The Nile is the second-longest river in the world. Its branches run through nine countries.

Map labels:

MOROCCO ☆ Rabat
Algiers ☆
Tunis ☆ Mediterranean
TUNISIA
Tripoli ☆
Atlas Mountains
Toubkal Peak
ALGERIA
LIBYA
Laayoune ●
WESTERN SAHARA (Claimed by Morocco)
Sahara Desert
Tropic of Cancer
3
MAURITANIA
MALI
NIGER
CHAD
Nouakchott ☆
Niger
Lake Chad
CAPE VERDE ☆ Praia
Dakar ☆ Sénégal
SENEGAL
Banjul ☆
GAMBIA
Bissau ☆
GUINEA-BISSAU
Bamako ☆
BURKINA FASO
Niamey ☆
Ouagadougou ☆
N'Djamena ☆
GUINEA
NIGERIA
Abuja ☆
Conakry ☆
IVORY COAST
GHANA
BENIN
TOGO
Freetown ☆
SIERRA LEONE
2
Porto-Novo ☆
Lagos ●
CAMEROON
CENTRAL AFRICAN REPUBLIC
Bangui ☆ Ubangi
Monrovia ☆
Yamoussoukro ☆
Accra ☆
Lomé
EQUATORIAL GUINEA
Malabo ☆
Yaounde ☆
Congo Basin
LIBERIA
SÃO TOMÉ & PRÍNCIPE
Sao Tome ☆
GABON
CONGO
DEMOCRATIC REPUBLIC OF THE CONGO
ATLANTIC OCEAN
Libreville ☆
Brazzaville ☆
Kasai
Kinshasa ☆
ANGOLA
5
Luanda ☆
ANGOLA
NAMIBIA
Windhoek ☆
Kalahari Desert
BOTSWANA
Orange
SOUTH AFRICA
Cape Town ☆ **5**
Cape of Good Hope

6

Ancient world

The pyramids at Giza in Egypt are believed to have been built more than 4,500 years ago. These amazing buildings were built as massive tombs for the Egyptian pharoahs.

Pyramids at Giza

Economy and environment

Tourism is very important to Kenya. Each year, millions of visitors take safaris to see many of the amazing wild animals such as lions, zebras, elephants, giraffes, and rhinoceroses.

7

Grevy's zebra

People and culture

A large number of ancient African tribes still live in the Omo Valley region of Ethiopia. These tribes, such as the Karo, Suri, and Hamar, still practice centuries-old customs, and many continue to wear traditional dress.

8

Omo Valley woman

9

Farming and agriculture

Madagascar produces and exports one-quarter of the world's vanilla. Each flower is **pollinated** by hand. After the flower has died, a fruit (pod) will grow. When this dries, vanilla's scent and flavor are released.

Vanilla flower and pods

Natural wonders

10

Mount Kilimanjaro is Africa's highest point. It contains three volcanoes. Two are extinct, while the other has been dormant for more than 200 years, but may erupt again in the future.

Mount Kilimanjaro

Mediterranean Sea
Suez Canal
Cairo
6
EGYPT
SAUDI ARABIA
Lake Nasser
Red Sea
Nile
SUDAN
Khartoum
White Nile
Blue Nile
ERITREA
Asmara
DJIBOUTI
Djibouti
Ethiopian Highlands
Addis Ababa
Horn of Africa
8
ETHIOPIA
SOUTH SUDAN
Juba
SOMALIA
N
KENYA
REPUBLIC CONGO
UGANDA
Kampala
7
Lake Victoria
Equator
Nairobi
Mogadishu
SEYCHELLES
Capital City
Victoria
Kigali
10
Mount Kilimanjaro
RWANDA
Bujumbura
BURUNDI
Dodoma
TANZANIA
Lake Tanganyika
Lake Nyasa (Lake Malawi)
COMOROS
Moroni
MAYOTTE (France)
Lilongwe
MALAWI
Zambezi
ZAMBIA
Lusaka
Victoria Falls
Harare
ZIMBABWE
9
Mozambique Channel
MADAGASCAR
Antananarivo
MAURITIUS
Port Louis
RÉUNION (France)
MOZAMBIQUE
Tropic of Capricorn
Gaborone
Pretoria
Maputo
SWAZILAND
Bloemfontein
Mbabane
LESOTHO
Maseru
INDIAN OCEAN

Northern Europe

Northern Europe has many different languages and cultures. This region can be split into three main areas. Estonia, Latvia, and Lithuania are called the Baltic States and were once part of the **Russian Empire**. Denmark, Sweden, Norway, Iceland, and Finland are called Scandinavia, an area that extends to the north as far as the Arctic Circle. England, Wales, Scotland, and Northern Ireland make up the United Kingdom.

Ancient world

1

The Vikings came from Norway, Sweden, and Denmark. They were skilled shipbuilders, and sailed to settle or trade throughout Europe and Asia. They crossed the Atlantic Ocean, reaching North America in 986 C.E.

Viking dragon head

National parks

2

Vatnajökull National Park

In Vatnajöökull National Park in Iceland is Europe's largest glacier. The ice cap is up to 0.6 miles (1 km) thick. Beneath the glacier, there are several still-active volcanoes.

Greenland Sea — *Arctic Circle* — *FAEROE ISLANDS (Denmark)*

ICELAND

Torshavn

Reykjavik — *Thjorsa* — **2** — *Hvannadalshnúkur*

Shetland Islands

Famous landmarks

Northern Ireland's Giant's Causeway consists of about 40,000 interlocking columns of basalt. It formed 50–60 million years ago when volcanic lava contracted, cracked and split during cooling.

Basalt columns, Giant's Causeway

Economy and environment

4

Denmark was a pioneer in developing wind power during the 1970s. The world's biggest wind turbine farms are just off Denmark's coast. The turbines provide 20% of the country's electricity.

Wind farm turbines

Outer Hebrides

Orkney Islands

Highlands ▲ *Ben Nevis*

ATLANTIC OCEAN

NORTHERN IRELAND

Glasgow — Edinburgh

3

SCOTLAND

Belfast

Nort Sea

UNITED KINGDOM

Shannon — *Irish Sea*

IRELAND — Dublin

Manchester

Cork — *WALES* — *ENGLAND*

Cardiff — Birmingham

N — *Celtic Sea* — *Thames* — London

Plymouth — **5**

English Channel

CHANNEL ISLANDS (UK)

FRANCE

Important buildings

5

Buckingham Palace is the main London home of the British royal family. The original house was built in 1703. When the queen is at home, her royal flag is flown from the top of the palace.

Buckingham Palace

ARCTIC OCEAN

North Cape

Barents Sea

Hammerfest

Lake Inari

Lapland

Kebnekaise

Arctic Circle

Kemijoki

NORWAY

SWEDEN

FINLAND

RUSSIAN FEDERATION

Norwegian Sea

Oulu

Lake Oulu

Trondheim

Jyväskylä

Lake Saimaa

Tampere

Gulf of Bothnia

7

Gidmå

Klaralven

Dalalven

Aland Islands

Turku

Helsinki

Bergen

10

Uppsala

Gulf of Finland

6

Tallinn

Lake Peipus

Oslo

Västerås

Hiiumaa

ESTONIA

Stavanger

Lake Vänern

Stockholm

Saaremaa

Lake Vättern

Gotland

Gulf of Riga

LATVIA

Skagerrak

Gothenburg

Öland

8

Riga

Western Dvina

DENMARK

Aalborg

4

Arhus

Copenhagen

Malmö

Baltic Sea

LITHUANIA

9

Vilnius

Odense

Bornholm

RUSS. FED.

BELARUS

POLAND

NETHERLANDS

GERMANY

Fact
Finland is called "The Land of the 1,000 Lakes." The country actually has close to 188,000 lakes!

**NUMBER OF COUNTRIES
10**

Sports and leisure

10

Ski jumping started in Scandinavia. Skiers are marked on the length and style of their jump. The sport has spread all over the world, but it is often the Norwegian and Finnish skiers who win the competitions.

Norwegian ski jumper

Music and festivals

6

Every five years, the Estonian Song Festival takes place in Tallinn. It is one of the world's largest choral events. Up to 30,000 singers entertain an audience of more than 80,000 people. The festival is held on the Tallinn Song Festival grounds.

Song Festival in Tallinn

King of Fjords, the Sognefjord

Natural wonders

7

A fjord is a narrow, steep-sided arm of the sea. It forms when seawater enters a valley once filled with a glacier. Norway's longest and deepest fjord is Sognefjord. It is 127 miles (205 km) long.

National symbols

The white wagtail is the national bird of Latvia. These birds are found in the country from April until October. These graceful birds often build nests in the rafters and eaves of buildings, stone piles, woodpiles, and birdhouses.

8

White wagtail

Nature and wildlife

9

Amber is fossilized sap (resin) of pine trees. Lithuania is famous for amber. A large river washed most of this amber out to the Baltic Sea millions of years ago from a pine forest.

Amber jewelry from Lithuania

Western Europe

This region of Europe is famous for its mountain ranges. The Alps stretch from France, Switzerland, and Germany all the way to Austria and Slovenia. The highest point, Mont Blanc, is more than 15,780 feet (4,800 m) tall. Germany has dense evergreen forests to the south and rolling hills in the north. The Netherlands and Belgium are both flat countries with many rivers and canals that provide ideal conditions for growing wheat, oats, and potatoes.

Music and festivals

1

The Belgian town of Binche has a huge annual carnival. A highlight is when masked performers, called Gilles, throw oranges to the crowds. An orange from a Gilles is a symbol of good luck!

Masked Gilles

Economy and environment

2

The Netherlands is famous for its many windmills. They were traditionally used for land drainage and to mill grain and timber. Of the 1,000 windmills that remain, some still carry out their function.

Windmill in the Netherlands

People and culture

3

A statue of the Austrian composer Wolfgang Amadeus Mozart stands in Salzburg, the city where he was born. Mozart died aged only 35, but his work included 17 masses, 24 operas, and more than 50 symphonies.

Mozart's statue

Map

North Sea

DENMARK

Baltic Sea

NETHERLANDS

Hamburg

GERMANY

Berlin

POLAND

2

The Hague · Amsterdam
Rotterdam
Elbe

Brussels

Essen
Cologne

Rhine

CZECH REPUBL

UNITED KINGDOM

English Channel

BELGIUM

1

Frankfurt am Main

LUXEMBOURG

Luxembourg

Danube

3

Linz

Seine

Paris

Strasbourg

4
Black Forest

Munich

Salzburg

AUSTRIA

V

5

Loire

SWITZERLAND

Innsbruck

Alps

Drava

Gr

N

Nantes

FRANCE

Zürich

Bern

LIECHTENSTEIN
Capital City
Vaduz

SLOVENI

Bay of Biscay

Lyon

Mont Blanc

Matterhorn

MONACO
Capital City
Monaco

ITALY

Massif Central

Rhône

Alps

SPAIN

Garonne

Toulouse
Balaïtous

Montpellier

Nice

Riviera

Ligurian Sea

Marseille

Pyrenees

Corsica

Fact
Liechtenstein is the smallest German-speaking country and the only one that doesn't border Germany.

NUMBER OF COUNTRIES
9

National parks

4

Germany's biggest nature reserve is the Black Forest. The region is full of pine and fir trees. The Danube, one of Europe's longest and most important rivers, begins in the Black Forest.

Black Forest

Famous landmarks

5

The Eiffel Tower is a huge iron structure in Paris. It was built in 1889 for the World's Fair. It is now the most popular tourist attraction in France. More than 250 million people have visited the tower.

Eiffel Tower

Eastern Europe

This region of Europe has been through a lot of changes during the last few decades. Czechoslovakia was split into the separate countries of Czechia (Czech Republic) and Slovakia. Similarly, the Soviet Union was dissolved, making Belarus and Ukraine independent countries. Two major rivers run through this region. The Dnieper flows through Russia, Belarus, and Ukraine into the Black Sea, while the Danube flows through ten countries.

1

Industry and technology

Many large cities in Czechia (Czech Republic) have trolley or streetcar networks. With 35 lines, the Prague network is the largest. Czech-made trolleys are exported around the world.

A tram in Prague

Sports and leisure

2

Poiana Brasov is a tourist center and ski resort in Romania. It is surrounded by four huge mountains that provide some very exciting ski runs for snowboarders and skiers of all abilities.

Snowboarder in Poiana Brasov

NUMBER OF COUNTRIES
9

Danube River in Budapest, Hungary

Fact
The Carpathian Mountains are about 932 miles (1,500 km) long. They form a semicircle, running through Czechia, Slovakia, Poland, Serbia, Hungary, Ukraine, and Romania.

Nature and wildlife

Bulgaria is home to the most stable population of brown bears in Europe. There are around 800 of these large wild animals living high up in the Rhodope Mountains in southwestern Bulgaria.

3

Sugar beet

Farming and agriculture

More than half of Poland is agricultural land. Poland grows more rye and potatoes than any other European country, and it is a prime producer of sugar beets, from which sugar is refined.

4

Brown bear

Rivers and lakes

5

The Danube is 1,777 miles (2,860 km) long and the second-longest river in Europe. It flows through four national capital cities and ten countries before emptying into the Black Sea in Ukraine and Romania.

19

Southern Europe

Each year, millions of tourists visit Southern Europe to enjoy the great weather, stunning scenery, and delicious food. Southern Europe consists of three peninsulas that reach out into the Mediterranean Sea. Spain and Portugal create the Iberian Peninsula. Italy, San Marino, and Vatican City form the Italian Peninsula, while the other countries to the east and the European part of Turkey belong to the Balkan Peninsula.

1 Nature and wildlife

The Iberian lynx is a highly endangered big cat. There could be only 300 of them left in the world. Charities in Portugal and Spain work together to breed the lynx in captivity, then reintroduce them into the wild.

Iberian lynx

National symbols 2

The *Galo de Barcelos* (Rooster of Barcelos) is a famous symbol of Portugal. The rooster is a symbol of honesty, integrity, and trust. Images of this brightly colored rooster are often seen on Portuguese handicrafts.

The *Galo de Barcelos*

NUMBER OF COUNTRIES
16

Bay of Biscay

FRANCE

Cantabrian Mts · Bilbao

ANDORRA
Capital City
Andorra la Vella

Braga
Porto
Duero · Valladolid
Ebro
Pyrenees
Monte Perdido
Gulf of Lion

PORTUGAL
SPAIN
Zaragoza
Barcelona

2
3 ★ Madrid
Tagus

Lisbon ★
Setúbal
Guadiana
Gulf of Valencia

Mallorca
Menorca

Valencia
Ibiza

Faro
Seville 1
Baetic Mts
Murcia
Formentera

Gulf of Cadiz
Málaga
Mulhacén
Mediterranean Sea

GIBRALTAR (UK)

SPAIN
PORTUGAL

AZORES (Portugal)

MADEIRA (Portugal)

CANARIES (Spain)

MOROCCO   ALGERIA

Sports and leisure

Real Madrid forward, Ronaldo

3

Real Madrid CF is Spain's most successful soccer team. They have won many titles. In 1920, King Alfonso XIII gave the club its "Real" (meaning royal) title and royal crown symbol.

Famous landmarks 4

Rome's Colosseum is a 2,000-year-old **amphitheater** that could hold more than 50,000 spectators. Dramas, executions, battle **reenactments**, and hunts were held here in Roman times (27 BCE–476 CE).

Colosseum

5 Music and festivals

The Carnival of Venice is held in Venice, Italy, each year. People wear masks to disguise themselves and enjoy the street theater, stilt walkers, and fire-eaters.

Carnival of Venice

6 Food and drink

Types of pasta

Italy is known for its pasta. Made from durum wheat, water, salt, and sometimes eggs, pasta can be formed into sheets, strands, ribbons, tubes, or shapes, or filled and folded to make stuffed pasta.

7 Natural wonders

Djavolja Varoš (Devil's Town)

Djavolja Varoš are ancient rock formations found in Serbia's Radan Mountains. They consist of 202 rock towers that were created millions of years ago by volcanic activity.

Farming and agriculture

8

Sunflowers are very important crops in Croatia. Their seeds can be eaten as a snack. Oil can be extracted from the seeds and used for cooking. The oil is also used to make biodiesel and margarine.

Sunflowers in Croatia

N

SWITZERLAND
AUSTRIA
Alps
ont
anc
SLOVENIA Maribor
HUNGARY
9
Lake Garda
Drava
Gran Paradiso
Milan
Ljubljana
Zagreb
8
ROMANIA
Venice
Po
CROATIA
Sava
Osijek
Novi Sad
Turin
Po Valley
5
Rijeka
Banja Luka
Bologna
Dalmatia
BOSNIA & HERZEGOVINA
Belgrade
Danube
iviera
Genoa
Apennines
Florence
Split
Sarajevo
SERBIA
Ligurian Sea
Nis
SAN MARINO
Capital City
San Marino
Tiber
Pristina
7
CORSICA
4
Podgorica
MONTENEGRO
KOSOVO
BULGARIA
Rome
ITALY
Skopje
VATICAN CITY
Capital City
Vatican City
Naples
Vesuvius
Bari
Adriatic Sea
Tirana
MACEDONIA
ALBANIA
Thessalonika
Sardinia
Tyrrhenian Sea
Mount Olympus
Larisa
TURKEY
Corfu
Lesbos
Cagliari
Palermo
Catanzaro
Ionian Sea
Pindus Mts
GREECE
Aegean Sea
Patras
Etna
Sicily
Catania
Athens
10
Dodecanese
Cyclades
Rhodes
Sea of Crete
TUNISIA
MALTA
Valletta
Crete
Iráklion

Fact
Vatican City is the smallest independent state in the world and the residence of the Pope, the leader of the Roman Catholic Church.

Mediterranean Sea

Mount Triglav

9

Parthenon

National parks

In Triglav National Park is Mount Triglav, the highest mountain in Slovenia. Triglav is a much-loved symbol. It is on the national crest and flag and on a coin. Slovenian soldiers once wore Triglav-shaped hats.

Ancient world 10

The Parthenon is an ancient temple. It was built 2,500 years ago on the Acropolis, a hill high above Athens. The temple honors Athena, goddess of inspiration, wisdom, and courage. Athens is also named for her.

Russian Federation

The Russian Federation is the largest country in the world. The west of the country is located in Europe, while the east lies in Asia. The landscape around the country varies dramatically. To the north there are frozen wastelands, which give way to vast dense forests. To the south the weather is warmer and land is cultivated. The far south, near the Mongolian border, has huge mountain ranges and hot dry deserts.

Famous landmarks

(5)

The Bronze Horseman is a nearly 20-foot (6-m) tall statue of Peter the Great. It is in the old capital of St. Petersburg. Tsar Peter was the first emperor of the Russian Empire. He died in 1725, but his reforms are still felt in modern Russia.

The Bronze Horseman statue

Sports and leisure

(1)

Rhythmic gymnastics originally began in Russia. It combines elements of ballet, gymnastics, and dance. Competitors are awarded points for their balances, **pirouettes**, leaps, and artistic presentation.

Rhythmic gymnastic routine

Important buildings

(2)

St. Basil's Cathedral, which was built in 1552, has nine uniquely shaped domes. It is a famous symbol of Russia. It is also recognized as a symbol of Moscow.

St. Basil's Cathedral

Fact
Russia was responsible for the first space flight and for launching the first satellite.

Food and drink

(3)

Caviar is a **luxury** food made from the eggs of the sturgeon fish. The best caviar is said to come from fish caught in the lakes and rivers of Russia. The Caspian Sea produces most of the world's caviar.

Black caviar

People and culture

(4)

The Bolshoi Ballet of Moscow and the Mariinsky Ballet of St. Petersburg are two of the world's most **respected** ballet companies. Ballet was first introduced to Russia from France more than 150 years ago.

Bolshoi Ballet

6

National parks

The Yugyd Va National Park is the largest of Russia's parks. This huge park contains the Ural Mountains and is home to mountain hares, flying squirrels, reindeer, and wolverines.

Yugyd Va National Park

Natural wonders

The Kamchatka Peninsula in eastern Russia has about 160 volcanoes, with 29 still active. The most striking volcano is the Kronotsky. At 11,571 feet (3,527 m), its classic cone is topped by a star-shaped glacier.

7

Kronotsky volcano

ARCTIC OCEAN

Chukchi Sea

Wrangel Island

East Siberian Sea

Severnaya Zemlya

New Siberian Islands

Laptev Sea

Arctic Circle

Anadyr

Bering Sea

Taymyr Peninsula

North Siberian Lowland

Kheta

Kotuy

Olenyok

oril'sk

Kolyma

Yana

Indigirka

Omolon

Magadan

Klyuchevskaya Sopka

7 Kamchatka Peninsula

Petropavlovsk-Kamchatskiy

S I B E R I A

Lena

Vilyuy

Yakutsk

Aldan

Sea of Okhotsk

Lower Tunguska

Chunya

Angara

Krasnoyarsk

Lena

Olekma

Vitim

Trans-Siberian Railway

Lake Baikal

10

Chita

Irkutsk

MONGOLIA

Argun

Amur

Khabarovsk

Ussuri

KURILE ISLANDS (Claimed by Japan)

Sakhalin

Yuzhno-Sakhalinsk

8

9

Vladivostok

Sea of Japan

JAPAN

CHINA

8

Siberian tiger

Industry and technology

The best way to see the stunning landscape of Russia is on the Trans-Siberian Railway. The main route runs from Moscow to Vladivostok. To ride the entire 5,772 miles (9,289 km) would take seven days.

9

Nature and wildlife

Russia's best known wild animal is the Siberian tiger. It is the largest cat in the world, with a 10-foot (3-m) body and 3-foot (1-m) tail. From near extinction, there are now 500 Siberians in eastern Russia.

Trans-Siberian Railway

Rivers and lakes

10

Lake Baikal is the world's oldest and deepest lake. It was created 30 million years ago and holds one-fifth of the world's fresh water. The lake provides nearly all of Russia's drinking water.

Lake Baikal

Southwest Asia

This area of Asia is the birthplace of three of the world's great religions: Judaism, Christianity, and Islam. The landscape is dramatic and diverse—from hot dry deserts where few animals or plants can survive to farmlands around rivers such as the Tigris and Euphrates in Turkey and Iraq. The most important resource in this area is oil, which has brought great wealth to several countries in this region.

1 Food and drink

Halloumi is a traditional cheese from Cyprus. It is made from a mixture of goat's milk and sheep's milk. In the warm months in Cyprus, it is traditional to eat grilled halloumi with watermelon.

A dish of halloumi cheese

NUMBER OF COUNTRIES 18

Famous landmarks

All Muslims face toward the Kaaba in Mecca, Saudi Arabia, during their daily prayers. The Kaaba—House of God—is a cube-shaped building in the center of the world's largest and most sacred mosque.

3

Kaaba in Mecca

Pamukkale in Turkey

2

Natural wonders

Pamukkale—Turkish for "cotton castle"— is a cascade of white terraces. They were formed slowly over thousands of years when calcium was deposited from the spring waters flowing over the cliff.

Fact

Some of the world's oldest villages were built near the Caspian Sea in Iran at least 6,000 years ago.

Map labels

RUSS. FED.
Black Sea
BULGARIA
Caucus Mts
Mount Kazbek
GEORGIA
Tbilisi
AZERBAIJAN
Baku
Caspian Sea
Koppeh Dagh
TURKMENISTAN
Istanbul
Bursa
Izmir
TURKEY
Ankara
Kızılırmak
ARMENIA
Yerevan
Tabriz
Elburz Mts
Mashhad
Lake Tuz
Taurus Mts
Lake Van
Lake Urmia
Mt Damavand
AFGHANISTAN
Adana
Tigris
Mosul
Tehran
2
Euphrates
IRAN
CYPRUS
1
Nicosia
SYRIA
IRAQ
Isfahan
PAKISTAN
LEBANON
Capital City
Beirut
Damascus
Baghdad
Zagros Mountains
Iranian Plateau
Amman
4
JORDAN
Basra
ISRAEL
Capital City
Jerusalem
KUWAIT
Kuwait City
Oman
An Nafud
SAUDI ARABIA
BAHRAIN
Capital City
Manama
QATAR
Doha
Abu Dhabi
Gulf of Oman
Muscat
Sur
Medina
Arabian Peninsula
Riyadh
Tropic of Cancer
UNITED ARAB EMIRATES
AFRICA
Black Sea
Jiddah
Mecca
3
Abha
Ar rub 'al Quarter (empty quarter)
5
Duqm
Arabian Sea
OMAN
Salalah
Sanaa
Al Mukalla
YEMEN
SOCOTRA (Yemen)
Ta'izz
Aden
Gulf of Aden
Persian Gulf
N

4 Ancient world

It is believed that the monastery in Petra was built for Nabatean king Obodas I, who reigned in the 1st century BCE. This huge ancient monument was carved directly into a mountain.

Monastery in Petra

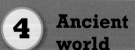

5 People and culture

The Bedouin people traditionally roamed the deserts. They moved from place to place, tending goats, sheep, and camels. Most Bedouins now live in towns, but some continue to live a nomadic desert life.

Bedouin herdsman

Central Asia

Central Asia covers a vast region with a varied geography, including high passes, mountains, and large deserts. There are extensive grassy plains, called steppes, running across this region and into Eastern Europe. The large mountain ranges covering Afghanistan, Tajikistan, and Kyrgyzstan are generally too dry or rugged to farm successfully, so most people in rural areas earn their living by herding livestock.

Nature and wildlife

1

The snow leopard is an endangered species of big cat that lives in the mountains of Central Asia. It is believed that there are between 180 and 220 of these secretive animals living in the forests of Tajikistan.

Snow leopard

Farming and agriculture

2

Threads of saffron

Over the last ten years, many farms in Afghanistan have started growing saffron. Saffron is one of the world's most expensive spices. It is used as a food flavoring, textile dye, and perfume scent.

Fact
Uzbekistan is double landlocked. This landlocked country is surrounded by countries that also have no access to the sea.

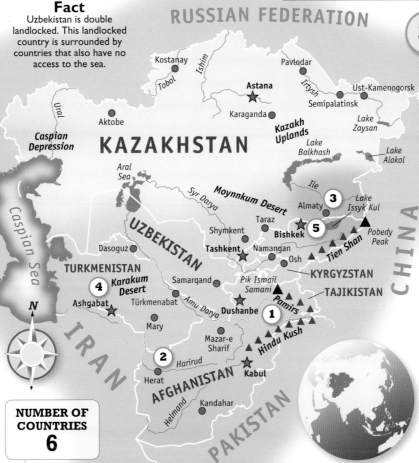

RUSSIAN FEDERATION

Kostanay
Astana
Pavlodar
Ust-Kamenogorsk
Tobol
Ishim
Irtysh
Semipalatinsk
Aktobe
Karaganda
Lake Zaysan
Caspian Depression
Kazakh Uplands
Lake Balkhash
Lake Alakol
KAZAKHSTAN
Aral Sea
Ural
Syr Darya
Moynnkum Desert
Ile
Lake Issyk Kul
Almaty **3**
Caspian Sea
Taraz
Bishkek **5**
Shymkent
Tien Shan
Pobedy Peak
UZBEKISTAN
Tashkent
Namangan
Osh
Dasoguz
CHINA
TURKMENISTAN
Samarqand
KYRGYZSTAN
Karakum Desert **4**
Pik Ismail Samani
TAJIKISTAN
Ashgabat
Türkmenabat
Amu Darya
Pamirs
N
Mary
Dushanbe **1**
Harirud
Mazar-e Sharif
Hindu Kush
2
Herat
Kabul
AFGHANISTAN
IRAN
Kandahar
Helmand
PAKISTAN

NUMBER OF COUNTRIES
6

Music and festivals

3

The dombra is a long-necked lute from Kazakhstan. It is played without a **plectrum** and strummed rapidly with the index finger. It was traditionally used to accompany epic poems and folk songs.

A traditional dombra

Deserts of the world

4

The Karakum Desert is one of the largest deserts in the world. It covers 80 percent of Turkmenistan. Its hot dry summers mean that only the toughest grasses, shrubs, bushes, and trees can grow here.

Karakum Desert

National parks

5

The Ala Archa is Kyrgyzstan's largest national park. It is in the Tien Shan range and has 20 glaciers and 50 peaks. The Ak-Sai and Adygene rivers originate from the melting waters of these glaciers.

Ala Archa National Park

South Asia

South Asia is surrounded by three bodies of water: the Bay of Bengal, the Indian Ocean, and the Arabian Sea. The vast landscape includes glaciers, rain forests, valleys, deserts, and grasslands. The climate changes from the extremely hot tropics in the south to cooler, drier weather in the north. This part of the world is the birthplace of many different religions, including Hinduism, Buddhism, Sikhism, and Jainism.

Sports and leisure

Cricket is not just the most popular sport in Pakistan, it is a passion. There are many **Test-grade** cricket grounds throughout Pakistan, and adults and children will use any patch of clear ground on which to play.

Pakistani cricketeer

NUMBER OF COUNTRIES
7

Important buildings

The Taj Mahal is India's best-loved attraction. Emperor Shah Jahan built it in memory of his wife Mumtaz Mahal. This white marble monument took more than 20 years to build and was completed in 1653.

The Taj Mahal

Rivers and lakes

The Ganges is the longest river in India. It flows all the way from the Himalayas across the plains of northern India to the Bay of Bengal in Bangladesh. Hindus consider the river holy and look upon it as a goddess.

Ganges River

AFGHANISTAN

Quetta

PAKISTAN

Central Makran Range

Mouths of the Indus

Hyderab

Karachi

Gulf of Kachch

Arabian Se

MALDIVES

Malé ☆

INDIAN OCEAN

Food and drink

Cinnamon originates from the island of Sri Lanka. This sweet-smelling spice is made from the inner bark of the cinnamon tree. It can be used in sweet and savory dishes and has many health benefits.

Cinnamon sticks and ground cinnamon

Famous landmarks

The Lotus Temple in New Delhi is open to all faiths and religions. It is an ideal place for meditation and finding peace and tranquility. Fifty million people have visited this temple!

Lotus Temple

6 National parks

The Sundarbans is the world's largest mangrove forest and a World Heritage Site. In the forest are 100 Bengal tigers. These tigers—equally agile in water as on land—are contained inside 56 miles (90 km) of fencing.

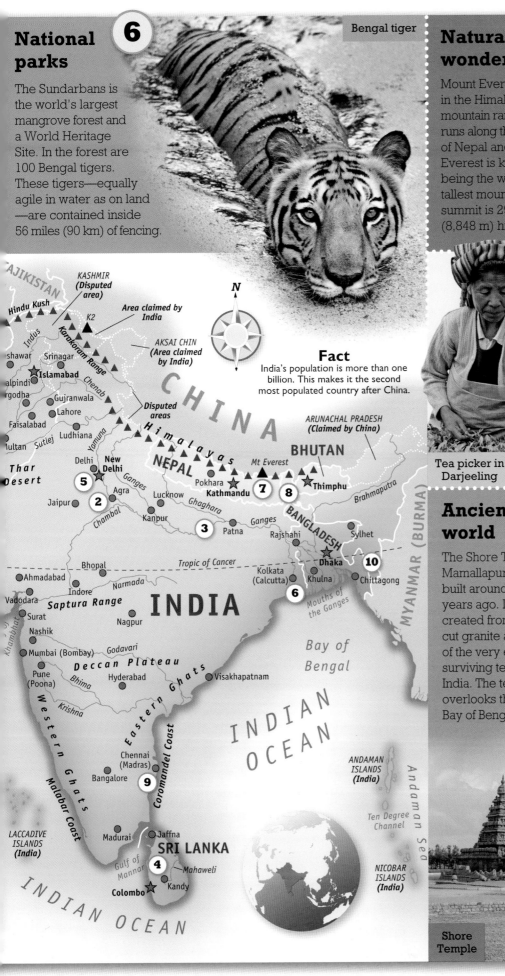

Bengal tiger

7 Natural wonders

Mount Everest is in the Himalaya mountain range, which runs along the border of Nepal and Tibet. Everest is known for being the world's tallest mountain. Its summit is 29,029 feet (8,848 m) high.

Mount Everest

8 Farming and agriculture

The Darjeeling district of India is famous for its exotic tea. The leaves are picked by hand from March until November. Only the very tips of the tea plant are picked to make this floral-smelling tea.

Tea picker in Darjeeling

Fact

India's population is more than one billion. This makes it the second most populated country after China.

Ancient world

The Shore Temple at Mamallapuram, was built around 1,300 years ago. It was created from finely cut granite and is one of the very earliest surviving temples in India. The temple overlooks the Bay of Bengal.

10

Indian peacock

National symbols

The national bird of India is the peacock. The males have beautiful iridescent plumage, and they shake their fanned-out tail feathers to attract a mate. The train feathers can be 6.6 feet (2 m) long.

9

Shore Temple

Map

TAJIKISTAN

Hindu Kush

KASHMIR (Disputed area)

Area claimed by India

K2

AKSAI CHIN (Area claimed by India)

Indus

Karakoram Range

Peshawar

Srinagar

Islamabad

rgodha

Chenab

Gujranwala

Lahore

Faisalabad

Ludhiana

ultan

Sutlej

Thar Desert

Delhi

New Delhi

5

Jaipur

2

Agra

Ganges

Yamuna

Chambal

Kanpur

3

Lucknow

Ghaghara

Patna

Ganges

CHINA

Disputed areas

Himalayas

NEPAL

Pokhara

7 8

Mt Everest

Kathmandu

ARUNACHAL PRADESH (Claimed by China)

BHUTAN

Thimphu

Brahmaputra

N

Bhopal

Tropic of Cancer

Rajshahi

BANGLADESH

Sylhet

Ahmadabad

Narmada

Indore

Vadodara

Saptura Range

Surat

Nashik

Mumbai (Bombay)

Godavari

Pune (Poona)

Bhima

Hyderabad

Nagpur

INDIA

Kolkata (Calcutta)

6

Khulna

Dhaka

10

Chittagong

Mouths of the Ganges

MYANMAR (BURMA)

Bay of Bengal

Deccan Plateau

Krishna

Eastern Ghats

Visakhapatnam

Western Ghats

Malabar Coast

Coromandel Coast

Bangalore

Chennai (Madras)

9

INDIAN OCEAN

ANDAMAN ISLANDS (India)

Andaman Sea

LACCADIVE ISLANDS (India)

Madurai

Jaffna

SRI LANKA

Gulf of Mannar

4

Mahaweli

Kandy

Colombo

Ten Degree Channel

NICOBAR ISLANDS (India)

INDIAN OCEAN

East Asia

East Asia is made up of six countries: China, Mongolia, Taiwan, North and South Korea, and Japan. China has a varied landscape including mountains, sandy beaches, and dense forests. Northern China and Mongolia suffer from severely cold winters. North Korea and South Korea form a peninsula with the Yellow Sea to the west, the East China Sea and Korea Strait to the south, and the Sea of Japan to the east.

Natural wonders **5**

Wulingyuan Scenic Area is famous for its 3,000 thin sandstone **pillars**, some more than 656 feet (200 m) tall. They formed when water, trapped in the rock, froze and expanded, causing chunks of rock to fall away.

Wulingyuan Scenic Area

People and culture **1**

Traditional nomadic people of Mongolia travel around the country tending to their animals. They live in felt-covered tents called yurts. These moveable homes protect them from harsh weather.

A Mongolian yurt

Music and festivals

New Year is a very important Chinese festival. Day one of the New Year aligns with a new moon between January 21 and February 20. There are fireworks, family gatherings, and good luck red envelopes (*hong baos*), containing money, are given to family and friends.

2

Red envelopes (hong baos)

Ancient world **3**

Construction of the Great Wall of China started in 221 BCE and was completed in 1644 CE. This hand-built stone-and-earth defensive structure snakes for 5,500 miles (8,852 km) over the mountains of China.

Great Wall of China

National symbols **4**

Giant pandas are the national animal of China. They spend most of their days eating bamboo. There are only around 1,860 of these large bears left living in the wild.

Giant pandas

NUMBER OF COUNTRIES
6

RUSSIAN

KAZAKHSTAN

Uvs Nuur

Altai Mountains

Irtysh

KYRGYZSTAN

Ile

Urumqi

Tien Shan

Tarim He

Area claimed by India

K2

Takla Makan Desert

Altan Shan

Kunlun Mountains

AKSAI CHIN (Area claimed by India)

Disputed areas

INDIA

NEPAL

Himalayas

Mt Everest

BHUTAN

Great Wall of China **3**

Qilian Shan

Qinghai Hu

Plateau of Tibet

TIBET

Salween

C H

Lhasa

Brahmaputra

ARUNACHAL PRADESH (Claimed by China)

MYANMAR (BURMA)

Mekong

N

Fact
The Yangtze River is the longest river in China. It is 3,915 miles (6,400 km) long, which makes it the third-longest river in the world.

6 Industry and technology

The *Shinkansen*, or bullet train, is a network of high-speed railway lines in Japan. The trains can reach speeds of 200 mph (320 kph) and are famous for their comfort, safety, and efficiency.

Shinkansen

Famous landmarks 7

The N Seoul Tower is a communications tower 777 feet (237 m) tall. It was built on top of a mountain in Seoul, South Korea. It features a revolving restaurant and decks with stunning views across the whole city.

N Seoul Tower

Deserts of the world 8

Bayanzag, or the Flaming Cliffs, is an area of the Gobi Desert famous for its yellow, orange, and red sand. The cliffs are rich in fossils, and it was here that dinosaur eggs were first found in 1922.

Bayanzag

Nature and wildlife 9

Rock macaques are small monkeys, native to the island of Taiwan. They live in large troops and make their homes in forests and grasslands. Their diet is made up of fruit, grass, leaves, insect, and birds' eggs.

Rock macaque mother and baby

10 National parks

Fuji-Hakone-Izu is the most visited of all of the Japanese national parks. The park contains Mount Fuji, Japan's largest mountain. Mount Fuji is known throughout the world as a symbol of Japan.

Mount Fuji

Map labels

EDERATION

Sühbaatar
Darhan
enet
Ulan Bator ★ 1
Choybalsan
MONGOLIA
Gobi Desert
andzadgad
Baotou
Yellow River
Beijing ★
Tianjin
Shijiazhuang
Taiyuan
Lanzhou
Zhengzhou
Wei Xi'an
A
Han Shui
Chengdu
Three Gorges Dam 5
ongqing
Yuan
ytze
Guiyang
nming
VIETNAM
Gulf of Tongking
Hainan Dao
South China Sea

Argun
Amur
Great Khingan range
Nen
Hegang
Hulun Nur
Qiqihar
Harbin
MANCHURIA
Jilin
Changchun
Fushun
Shenyang
Haicheng Yalu
Dalian
Tangshan
Zibo
Jinan
Qingdao
Xuzhou
Huai
Nanjing
Wuhan Yangtze
Hangzhou
Nanchang
Changsha
Tizi
Xiang
Gan
Fuzhou
Xi Jiang
Guangzhou
Tropic of Cancer
Kaohsiung
Hong Kong 2
Taipei ★ 9
TAIWAN

Ussuri
Lake Khanka
NORTH KOREA
Hamhung
Pyongyang ★
Seoul ★ 7
SOUTH KOREA
Pusan
Yellow Sea
Shanghai
East China Sea

Sea of Okhotsk
KURILE ISLANDS (Claimed by Japan)
Hokkaido
Sapporo
JAPAN
Sendai
Honshu
Mount Fuji 10 Tokyo
Yokohama
Kobe Nagoya
Hiroshima Osaka
Shikoku
Kyushu
6 Kagoshima
Ryukyu Islands (Japan)
PACIFIC OCEAN
Philippine Sea
Sea of Japan

29

Southeast Asia

Southeast Asia lies south of China and east of India. Malaysia, the Philippines, Indonesia, and Brunei make up the long lines of islands that stretch eastwards into the Pacific Ocean. Much of Southeast Asia is made up of thick rain forest where elephants, tigers, and exotic lizards can be found. The hot and wet climate in most of this region provides ideal conditions for growing rice, one of the main foods grown here.

1 Music and festivals

Each year in April, Thailand celebrates Songkran, the Thai New Year. This festival falls in the middle of the hottest part of the year, so fun water fights are held in parks and streets throughout the country.

Songkran, New Year festival

2 Important buildings

The Petronas Twin Towers, in Malaysia's capital city, Kuala Lumpur, are the tallest twin buildings in the world. There is a sky bridge that connects the two towers on the 41st and 42nd floors.

Petronas Twin Towers

3

Taman Negara rainforest

4 Food and drink

Laksa is a popular Singaporean dish that blends Chinese and Malaysian flavors. It consists of a spicy soup (often made with coconut milk), rice noodles, herbs, and fish, prawns, or chicken.

Prawn laksa

National parks

The ancient tropical rain forest in Taman Negara is about 130 million years old. This national park in Malaysia is home to wild pigs, leopards, sun bears, Sumatran rhinoceroses, tapirs, and tigers.

Ancient world

Angkor Wat is a complex of more than 100 ancient stone temples in Cambodia. The temples were built more than 1,200 years ago. It is the world's largest religious construction, and the most popular tourist attraction in Cambodia.

Angkor Wat

NUMBER OF COUNTRIES 11

Map labels:
Hkakabo Razi
INDIA
CHINA
Tropic of Cancer
Chindwin
Irrawaddy
Myitkyina
Monywa
Mandalay
Chauk
MYANMAR (BURMA)
Salween
Sittwe
Taunggyi
LAOS
Black River
Red River
Thai Nguyen
Hai Phong
Naypyidaw
Hanoi
Prome
Chiang Mai
Bago
Vientiane
Gulf of Tongking
Pathein
Rangoon
Mawlamyine
Udon Thani
VIETNAM
Hue
Mouths of the Irrawaddy
Nakhon Ratchasima
Da Nang
Dawei
THAILAND
Bangkok
Can Tho
CAMBODIA
ANDAMAN ISLANDS (India)
Tonle Sap
Nha Trang
Ho Chi Minh
Phnom Penh
Andaman Sea
Isthmus of Kra
Gulf of Thailand
Ko Samui
Can Tho
Mouths of the Mekong
NICOBAR ISLANDS (India)
Mekong
Phuket
Hat Yai
Malay Peninsula
Kota Bharu
Natuna Islands
George Town
Kuala Terengganu
Ipoh
Strait of Malacca
Kuala Lumpur
MALAY
Medan
SINGAPORE
Capital City Singapore
Kuching
Singkawang
Equator
Pontianak
Kapuas
Sumatra
Padang
Jambi
Bangka
Greater
BARISAN MOUNTAINS
Palembang
Mentawai Islands
Bandar Lampung
I   N
Jakarta
Semarang
Bandung
Java
Yogyakarta
N
INDIAN

6 Natural wonders

Vietnam's Halong Bay has thousands of **islets** and **pillars** topped with forests. The bay's emerald, green water laps into hidden **grottoes** and against floating villages. It is a World Heritage Site.

Halong Bay

Coconuts

7 National symbols

The Indian elephant is the national animal of Laos. These large animals live in the forested areas of the country. They have smaller heads and larger trunks than African elephants.

Indian elephant

Farming and agriculture

The Philippines leads the world in coconut production. Coconut flesh is eaten, its milk drunk, and its oil used in cosmetics and cooking. The husks are woven into **coir** ropes and the flowers have **medicinal** uses.

8

Famous landmarks 9

In Bandar Seri Begawan, the capital city of Brunei, there is a royal mosque. It has marble columns, a large dome covered in pure gold and a huge, beautiful prayer hall that can hold up to 3,000 worshippers.

Omar Ali Saifuddien Mosque

Nature and wildlife

Wild orangutans are only found in the rain forests on the islands of Borneo and Sumatra. They sleep in nests in the trees, and live on a diet of young leaves, fruit, bark shoots, insects, birds' eggs, and honey.

10

Fact
The islands of Indonesia have more active volcanoes than any other country in the world.

Luzon Strait

Luzon

Baguio

Manila ☆

PHILIPPINES 8

Mindoro

Panay

Iloilo

Palawan

Samar

Cebu

Negros

Mindanao

Zamboanga

Davao

South China Sea

Sulu Sea

Philippine Sea

PACIFIC OCEAN

BRUNEI
Capital City
Bandar Seri
Begawan

9

Kinabalu ▲

Kota
Kinabalu

Sandakan

Sulu Archipelago

Celebes Sea

Manado

Halmahera

Borneo

Samarinda

10

Barito

Balikpapan

Palu

Makassar Strait

Sulawesi

Molucca Sea

MOLUCCAS

unda Islands

Banjarmasin

Parepare

Buru

Seram

Ambon

I N D O N E S I A

ava Sea

Makassar

Banda Sea

Aru Islands

Puncak
Jaya ▲

Central
Range

Papua

Mamberamo

Jayapura

PAPUA
NEW
GUINEA

urabaya

Flores Sea

Semeru ▲

lang

Mataram

Lesser Sunda Islands

Flores

Savu Sea

Dili ☆

**EAST
TIMOR**

A r a f u r a   S e a

Bali

Lombok

Sumba

Sumbawa

Timor

Kupang

*Timor
Sea*

OCEAN

Orangutan

Australia

Australia is a huge country and the world's largest island. It is the only country that is classified as a continent. A third of the land is made up of hot, dry desert. The scorching temperatures and lack of water make it tough for vegetation or animals to thrive there. Most people live in the south where the weather is cooler. Australia has many animals that are not found elsewhere, such as platypuses, kangaroos, and koalas.

Famous landmarks **1**

The Broken Hill Sculpture Symposium is a tourist attraction in the Australian outback. The park was created in 1993, when 12 artists from around the world were commissioned to create sandstone sculptures.

Broken Hill Symposium

Nature and wildlife **2**

Kangaroos are the most well-known Australian animals. They have powerful hind legs, a long, strong tail, and small front legs. They are herbivorous, so they eat grasses, shrubs, and some fungi.

Red kangaroo

Great Barrier Reef

Natural wonders **3**

The Great Barrier Reef is the world's largest reef system. It is home to amazing wildlife, including some vulnerable and endangered species, such as seahorses, sea snakes, dugongs, and marine turtles.

NUMBER OF STATES 6

Fact
Australia's main exports are iron ore, coal, gold, natural gas, beef, aluminium ores, and wheat.

Important buildings **4**

The Sydney Opera House has five theaters, and many studios and rehearsal rooms. It is one of the world's most famous buildings and one of the most respected performing arts **venues**.

Sydney Opera House

People and culture **5**

The largest population of Indigenous peoples in Australia is found in New South Wales. Indigenous culture in Australia is kept alive through art, dance, music, and traditional storytelling.

Indigenous art

New Zealand and the Pacific Islands

The Pacific Islands are a group of islands that are sometimes called Oceania. Many different cultures and languages can be found on the islands. New Zealand is a remote group of islands. Its closest neighbor is Australia, which is more than 1,240 miles (2,000 km) away. The main islands of New Zealand, the North and South Islands, are separated by the Cook Strait, which connects the Tasman Sea with the South Pacific Ocean.

Nature and wildlife

1

The Marshall Islands are popular with divers because of their ocean wildlife. The world's largest shark sanctuary was created there in 2011 to protect the sharks and ocean life around the islands.

Gray reef shark

Economy and environment

Called the "home of happiness," the Republic of Fiji has 333 islands. Tourists flock there to enjoy white sandy beaches, coconut palm trees, coral reefs, warm climate, mountains, and tropical forests.

People and culture

3

Papua New Guinea is home to 700 different Indigenous tribes. More languages are spoken there than in any other country in the world. Tribal identities and traditions remain essential to Papuans.

Traditional dress of Papuan tribe

Sports and leisure

4

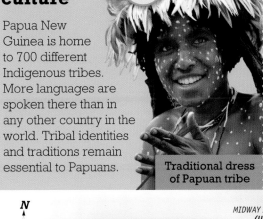
New Zealand rugby player

Rugby is the most-followed sport in New Zealand. It is a tough game where two teams of 15 players compete to place an oval ball over the goal line or to kick it between two goal posts.

White sandy beach, Fiji

2

Map

N

Tropic of Cancer

MIDWAY ISLANDS *(US)*

HAWAIIAN ISLANDS *(US)*

NORTHERN MARIANA ISLANDS *(US)*

WAKE ISLAND *(US)*

JOHNSTON ATOLL *(US)*

GUAM *(US)*

MARSHALL ISLANDS

NORTH PACIFIC OCEAN

PALAU

MICRONESIA

BAKER & HOWLAND ISLANDS *(US)*

KINGMAN REEF *(US)*

PALMYRA ATOLL *(US)*

JARVIS ISLAND *(US)*

Equator

INDONESIA

PAPUA NEW GUINEA

Mount Wilhelm ▲

3

NAURU

SOLOMON ISLANDS

KIRIBATI

TOKELAU *(New Zealand)*

KIRIBATI

Port Moresby ☆

TUVALU

AMERICAN SAMOA *(US)*

WALLIS & FUTUNA *(France)*

Coral Sea

VANUATU

2

SAMOA

COOK ISLANDS *(New Zealand)*

FRENCH POLYNESIA *(France)*

TONGA

NEW CALEDONIA *(France)*

FIJI

NIUE *(New Zealand)*

Tropic of Capricorn

PITCAIRN ISLANDS *(UK)*

NORFOLK ISLAND *(Australia)*

KERMADEC ISLANDS *(New Zealand)*

Fact
The Indigenous Maori peoples migrated to New Zealand sometime in the last 700 to 2,000 years.

Tasman Sea

North Island

4

NEW ZEALAND

Aoraki (Mount Cook) ▲

☆ Wellington

5

South Island

CHATHAM ISLANDS *(New Zealand)*

Stewart Island

CAPITAL CITIES NOT SHOWN ON MAP	
Country	**Capital City**
Fiji	Suva
Kiribati	Tarawa
Marshall Islands	Majuro
Micronesia	Palikir
Nauru	*No official capital*
Palau	Ngerulmud
Samoa	Apia
Solomon Islands	Honiara
Tonga	Nuku'alofa
Tuvalu	Funafuti
Vanuatu	Port Vila

NUMBER OF COUNTRIES 13

Farming and agriculture

5

Sheep farming is one of the biggest industries in New Zealand, which has about 30 million sheep. Most farms are on the South Island, where sheep outnumber humans by six to one!

Sheep in New Zealand

Countries and capital cities of the world

A
Afghanistan, Kabul 25
Albania, Tirana 21
Algeria, Algiers 14
Andorra, Andorra la Vella 20
Angola, Luanda 14
Antigua & Barbuda, St. John's 11
Argentina, Buenos Aires 13
Armenia, Yerevan 24
Australia, Canberra 32
Austria, Vienna 18
Azerbaijan, Baku 24

B
Bahamas, Nassau 11
Bahrain, Manama 24
Bangladesh, Dhaka 27
Barbados, Bridgetown 11
Belarus, Minsk 19
Belgium, Brussels 18
Belize, Belmopan 11
Benin, Porto-Novo 14
Bhutan, Thimphu 27
Bolivia, La Paz, Sucre, 12
Bosnia and Herzegovina, Sarajevo 21
Botswana, Gaborone 15
Brazil, Brasília 13
Brunei, Bandar Seri Begawan 31
Bulgaria, Sofia 19
Burkina Faso, Ouagadougou 14
Burundi, Bujumbura 15

C
Cambodia, Phnom Penh 30
Cameroon, Yaounde 14
Canada, Ottawa 7
Cape Verde, Praia 14
Central African Republic, Bangui 14
Chad, N'Djamena 14
Chile, Santiago 12
China, Beijing 29
Colombia, Bogotá 12
Comoros, Moroni 14
Congo, Brazzaville 14
Costa Rica, San José 11
Croatia, Zagreb 21
Cuba, Havana 11
Cyprus, Nicosia 24
Czechia (Czech Republic), Prague 19

D
Democratic Republic of the Congo, Kinshasa 14
Denmark, Copenhagen 17
Djibouti, Djibouti 15
Dominica, Roseau 11
Dominican Republic, Santo Domingo 11

E
East Timor, Dili 31
Ecuador, Quito 12
Egypt, Cairo 15
El Salvador, San Salvador 11
Equatorial Guinea, Malabo 14
Eritrea, Asmara 15
Estonia, Tallinn 17
Ethiopia, Addis Ababa 15

F
Fiji, Suva 33
Finland, Helsinki 17
France, Paris 18
French Guiana, Cayenne 13

G
Gabon, Libreville 14
Gambia, Banjul 14
Georgia, Tbilisi 24
Germany, Berlin 18
Ghana, Accra 14
Greece, Athens 21
Grenada, St. George's 11
Guatemala, Guatemala City 11
Guinea, Conakry 14
Guinea-Bissau, Bissau 14
Guyana, Georgetown 13

H
Haiti, Port-au-Prince 11
Honduras, Tegucigalpa 11
Hungary, Budapest 19

I
Iceland, Reykjavik 16
India, New Delhi 27
Indonesia, Jakarta 30
Iran, Tehran 24
Iraq, Baghdad 24
Ireland, Dublin 16
Israel, Jerusalem 24
Italy, Rome 21
Ivory Coast, Yamoussoukro 14

J
Jamaica, Kingston 11
Japan, Tokyo 29
Jordan, Amman 24

K
Kazakhstan, Astana 25
Kenya, Nairobi 15
Kiribati, Tarawa 33
Kosovo, Pristina 21
Kuwait, Kuwait City 24
Kyrgyzstan, Bishkek 25

L
Laos, Vientiane 30
Latvia, Riga 17
Lebanon, Beirut 24
Lesotho, Maseru 15
Liberia, Monrovia 14
Libya, Tripoli 14
Liechtenstein, Vaduz 18
Lithuania, Vilnius 17
Luxembourg, Luxembourg 18

M
Macedonia, Skopje 21
Madagascar, Antananarivo 15
Malawi, Lilongwe 15
Malaysia, Kuala Lumpur 30
Maldives, Malé 26
Mali, Bamako 14
Malta, Valletta 21
Marshall Islands, Majuro 33
Mauritania, Nouakchott 14
Mauritius, Port Louis 15
Mexico, Mexico City 10
Micronesia, Palikir 33
Moldova, Chisinau 19
Monaco, Monaco 18
Mongolia, Ulan Bator 9
Montenegro, Podgorica 21
Morocco, Rabat 14
Mozambique, Maputo 15
Myanmar (Burma), Naypyidaw 30

N
Namibia, Windhoek 14
Nauru, No official capital 33
Nepal, Kathmandu 27
Netherlands Amsterdam 18 The Hague 18
New Zealand, Wellington 33
Nicaragua, Managua 11
Niger, Niamey 14
Nigeria, Abuja 14
North Korea, Pyongyang 29
Norway, Oslo 17

O
Oman, Muscat 24

P
Pakistan, Islamabad 27
Palau, Ngerulmud 33
Panama, Panama City 11
Papua New Guinea, Port Moresby 33
Paraguay, Asunción 13
Peru, Lima 12
Philippines, Manila 31
Poland, Warsaw 19
Portugal, Lisbon 20

Q
Qatar, Doha 24

R
Romania, Bucharest 19
Russian Federation, Moscow 22
Rwanda, Kigali 15

S
Samoa, Apia 33
San Marino, San Marino 21
São Tomé & Príncipe, Sao Tome 14
Saudi Arabia, Riyadh 24
Senegal, Dakar 14
Serbia, Belgrade 21
Seychelles, Victoria 15
Sierra Leone, Freetown 14
Singapore, Singapore 30
Slovakia, Bratislavia 19
Slovenia, Ljubljana 21
Solomon Islands, Honiara 33
Somalia, Mogadishu 15
South Africa, Bloemfontein, 15 Cape Town 14 Tshwane 15
South Korea, Seoul 29

S (continued)
South Sudan, Juba 15
Spain, Madrid 20
Sri Lanka, Colombo 27
St. Kitts & Nevis, Basseterre 11
St. Lucia, Castries 11
St. Vincent & the Grenadines, Kingstown 11
Sudan, Khartoum 15
Suriname, Paramaribo 13
Swaziland, Mbabane 15
Sweden, Stockholm 17
Switzerland, Bern 18
Syria, Damascus 24

T
Taiwan, Taipei 29
Tajikistan, Dushanbe 25
Tanzania, Dodoma 15
Thailand, Bangkok 30
Togo, Lomé 14
Tonga, Nuku'alofa 33
Trinidad and Tobago, Port-of-Spain 11
Tunisia, Tunis 14
Turkey, Ankara 24
Turkmenistan, Ashgabat 25
Tuvalu, Funafuti 33

U
Uganda, Kampala 15
Ukraine, Kyiv 19
United Arab Emirates, Abu Dhabi 24
United Kingdom, London 16
United States of America, Washington D.C. 9
Uruguay, Montevideo 13
Uzbekistan, Tashkent 25

V
Vanuatu, Port Vila 33
Vatican City, Vatican City 21
Venezuela, Caracas 12
Vietnam, Hanoi 30

Y
Yemen, Sanaa 24

Z
Zambia, Lusaka 15
Zimbabwe, Harare 15

Learning more

Books

Basher, Simon, *Countries of the World: An Atlas with Attitude*, Kingfisher, 2018

Kalman, Bobbie, *Spotlight on the United States of America*, Crabtree, 2008

Lonely Planet Kids, *The Travel Book: A journey through every country in the world*, Lonely Planet Kids, 2015

Panta, Mark, *Countries of the World: Trivia of all countries in the world*, CreateSpace, 2014

Spotlight on (series). Crabtree, 2008–2013.

Websites

www.atozkidsstuff.com/world.html
Things to know about every country in the world and things to do there. Countries are divided by continent.

www.ducksters.com/geography
Maps, flags, and lots of information about each country.

www.factmonster.com/countries
Facts and figures about each country, including the government, economy, and people.

https://kids.nationalgeographic.com/search-results/?q=countries
Information about the geography, history, government, nature, and people of the world's countries.

www.kids-world-travel-guide.com/geography-facts.html
Lots of facts and information about the world's continents, countries, and people.

www.sciencekids.co.nz/sciencefacts/countries.html
Provides interesting trivia and information about the countries of the world.

Glossary

amphitheater A roofless building with tiers of seats for spectators and a central space for presentation of plays or sporting events

archipelago A stretch of sea or water containing many islands

coir Fiber from the outer husks of coconuts, used for making ropes and mats

descendants The children, grandchildren, etc., of a particular ancestor

economy The wealth and resources of a country or region, especially in goods and services

erosion The gradual wearing away of something by the actions of wind, rain, or water

exceptional Unusual; not typical; outstanding

export To send to another country to be sold there

geological activity Processes such as pressure and volcanic activity that change and form rock

grottoes A small scenic cave, often created over water

Indigenous Originating from or naturally occurring in a particular place; native

inscriptions Words or symbols written on or carved into something as a permanent record

inuksuit Plural form of inukshuk; stone figures used by Inuit peoples to guide the way for travelers and hunters

islet A small island

krill Tiny shrimplike animals that live in open seas, usually eaten by whales

medicinal Having healing properties

native Born or naturally growing in a specific place

navigation aids Objects or signs that help travelers know which direction they are heading

ornate Having a lot of complicated decoration

pillars Tall thin natural rock structures

pirouettes The act of spinning on one foot with the other foot raised off the ground

plectrum A small flat piece of plastic, wood, or other flexible material used to pluck the strings of an instrument

pollinated To carry pollen to or deposit it on a plant to fertilize it

predator An animal that hunts, kills, and eats other animals

reenactment The acting out of a historical event, such as a battle

rhythmic Having a strong, regular, repeated pattern of movement or sound

Russian Empire An empire consisting of Tsarist Russia and the territories it governed in Europe and Asia from 1712–1917

sea level The level of the sea's surface, which is used to determine the height of geological features such as mountains and hills

symbol Something that represents or stands for a particular idea, object, or relationship, such as a country or a value

symbolic Serving as a symbol

Test-grade A very long type of cricket match that is physically and mentally challenging

venue A place where an organized event, such as a concert or sporting event, takes place

Index